Fence, Patio, Blessed Virgin

poems by

Kristin Brace

Finishing Line Press
Georgetown, Kentucky

Fence, Patio, Blessed Virgin

Copyright © 2018 by Kristin Brace
ISBN 978-1-63534-603-9 First Edition
All rights reserved under International and Pan-American Copyright Conventions. No part of this book may be reproduced in any manner whatsoever without written permission from the publisher, except in the case of brief quotations embodied in critical articles and reviews.

ACKNOWLEDGMENTS

Gratitude to Rob Kenagy for his vision and feedback on an early draft.

All poems previously unpublished.

Publisher: Leah Maines
Editor: Christen Kincaid
Cover Art: Meridith Ridl
Author Photo: Neal Brace
Cover Design: Elizabeth Maines McCleavy

Printed in the USA on acid-free paper.
Order online: www.finishinglinepress.com
        also available on amazon.com

        Author inquiries and mail orders:
            Finishing Line Press
             P. O. Box 1626
        Georgetown, Kentucky 40324
               U. S. A.

Table of Contents

I.	1
a)	2
II.	3
b)	4
III.	5
c)	6
IV.	7
d)	8
V.	9
e)	10
VI.	11
f)	12
VII.	13
g)	14
VIII.	15
h)	16
IX.	17
i)	19
X.	21
j)	22
XI.	23
k)	24
XII.	25

I.

In April, we take the Buick
around the bottom of the lake,
Mom driving, me sitting cross-
legged in the front seat. I think
how tired and angry and scattered
I am, somebody's name
sparkler-sprawled on a dark
July night. My lips think *how soft
my grandma's cheek* (fizzle softens
to firefly, shoulders soften to seat).
Tomorrow's kiss gets me through
Gary. She's nearing ninety-seven,
wears compression socks pulled on
what seems like thread by thread.
"Painful to watch," Mom says.
Now, behind the wheel, the bridge
of her nose is stitched down with all
the things that don't have words. We listen
to Elton John and Fleetwood Mac.
You can go your own way, we sing
while we swoop up to Madison
for my sister. On a map, we'd be a starling,
startled, wings spread, color of a deep
river at dusk, muddy in flood season.
I can't remember if starlings stay all year,
or if they migrate and return,
the old birds blurring into the new.

a)

*I'm thirteen, all glasses and braces,
breasts nonexistent, hips of a boy.
But I'm wearing my grandma's dress,
posing in the sunroom between
my sister and cousin, the carpet's
familiar textured feel, faintly plasticky,
beneath my feet. A peachy sunlit
afternoon—date and time, unimportant.
Turning and posing among ourselves
and for our mothers. The older girls
wear semi-formal 50s frocks that hit
above the knee, thick and silky well-
tailored numbers, pearly blue and deep
chocolatey brown with bronze sheen.
Hands on well-formed hips—turn—
giggle—turn. Our mothers laugh
as they always do and ooh and ahh
on the gliding loveseat. It creaks
and creaks. The overhead fan wobbles
and clicks as it turns, turns. For me,
a long green house dress, soft fabric
that ripples across my legs as I walk.
I walk to feel that feeling, no place to go.
The dress is from the 60s or 70s, brilliant
pink and pool-blue flowers bursting
against the artificial green. I'll keep
this dress, find it tucked along the side
of my closet in my thirties with the other
clothes I never wear and will never discard.
Creak, click, wobble, strut, turn, giggle.
"Can you imagine what Grandma
looked like in these?" we ask, beaming.
We call to her: Grandma, come and see.
The sunroom not a mirror, exactly.
And my memory hazy as to if or when
she appeared. But we harbored no doubt
that she would: she was always there.*

II.

We have too much luggage for three people,
a pile of pillows, a backseat
pyramid of sweaters and bags.
Tortilla chip crumbs gather in crevices
of the plush maroon seats.
It's us, our stuff, our detritus.
The thing we become when we are all three.
The Buick is our boat, sailing us northwest
past Sun Prairie, Baraboo, the Dells.
Charmed by sunshine, by getting away,
for a while we forget how to fight. Someone
is cranked around in their seat, similar teeth
bared and noses flared with laughter.
Farther north, the earth gathers itself
in squat hills of sumptuous green.
Holsteins graze and rock face runs
with late melting snow. How changed
will she be when we arrive? Eau Claire
means an hour to go, means
happy legs and when will we get theres,
snappy comments and hunching in seats.
It means we're closer to something sacred.
The fear of not finding what we find elusive
for awhile, at least, can't find us.

b)

Gratitude for not knowing the future.
Not knowing that by next April,
Grandma will have spent two months
in assisted living. She'll have fallen
out of bed multiple times, they'll have
painted her nails a garish red.
Visiting for her ninety-eighth birthday in July,
we find her with an ugly gash in her arm,
alarmingly hunched in her wheelchair
and unable to stay awake. We wait
for the transport service to take her
to the hospital, we tuck her in
with pillows so she doesn't topple forward,
so she doesn't have to labor so hard to breathe.
My husband folds a sweater around her shoulders.
A caretaker says in her ear, "Can I get you
anything, Rose?" She replies, "I'd sure like
some work to do," and falls back asleep.
We watch her breathing. We wait.
We touch her shoulder, hold her hands,
careful not to disturb her injured arm.
Another caretaker stoops beside her and asks
loudly, "Rose, how do you feel?" Grandma
opens her eyes and says, "With my fingers,"
and her head dips in sleep again.

III.

We didn't go last summer.
We missed barefoot kickball,
cartwheels in the yard, two fridges full
and bellies fuller. We missed the uncle
who maybe wouldn't come and lips
drawn tight over girlhood envy grown.
We missed Grandma asking
for just a sliver more. We missed how dark
it gets at night. While toads made their
damp way across the drive, I used to sing
in that cleanest garage where for longer
than I've been alive, we've celebrated
her birthday. In there alone, it was like
a giant shower, all echoes. Even if time
could fit like a cardinal in your hands,
every year just another bright feather,
you couldn't compress all those birthdays
into just two stalls. A song, a joke,
an impromptu polka, a clink of glasses
and a shouted *Na zdrowie!*—something
would flutter free. How quiet it will be,
arriving in spring. How quietly she must wait,
if she remembers we're coming.

c)

*Grandma walks the rosary every day,
exercise and prayers accomplished
in efficient circuits through the house.
Hail Mary past the kitchen counter
where she teaches my sister and me—
clad in shiny pink leotards, resisting
the urge to spin on our stools—how
to make her famous sweet rolls
with maple frosting. Hail Mary
past the freezer where she stores them
by the dozen in stiff cereal bags
salvaged one by one from the box.
Hail Mary past the closet with rags
labeled "bad" and "good," Mary
full of grace and the washer full
of clothes. Her fingers worry
the clear blue beads, her mouth shaping
and reshaping the familiar words.
The Lord is with thee. Clean white
tennis shoes across the clean floor.
"Grandma's walking," Mom says,
and we know not to get in her way.
She carries her concentration with her,
quiets our play with her reverence worn
like a shawl by the air she stirs.
Sometimes, we can't help ourselves—
we catch her eye, we make silly faces.
We break the halo of silence
and she grins at us, maybe even chuckles.
Blessed art thou among women
and blessed is the fruit of thy womb.*

IV.

Closer to Grandma's, I never remember
the names of the roads curving through
cornfields (all letters and numbers, quarters
and eighths of miles from the county line),
but, driving now, I follow them intuitively.
We pass lakeside bars, a cemetery spotted
with sprays of fake flowers, spent
pussy willows, a peeling barn. Breath
comes easier. Highway 8 threads straight
as a needle through brush and white pine.
My foot presses harder on the gas.
Left on her gravel road, left
on her driveway. The house looks tired.
I squint at the kitchen window,
where we used to see her face peering,
grin stretching wide when she was sure it was us.
The window is blank, a slash of sky.
We find the hidden key and enter.
She's been dozing. There's a flat spot
in her hair. She's shorter. More stooped.
She walks only with the walker that,
last year, she refused. Such tenderness,
then, in my very bones, when I hear
her little chuckle, like a chicken's cluck.

d)

*In the years before praying
through the house, she walks the yard,
along the treeline to the east
and south, back along the house
to the garden brimming with lettuce,
garlic, zinnias, dill, past the white
potting shed and bushes dense
with raspberries. Then north along the edge
of the woods back of the house,
the yard patterned with patches
of yellow birdsfoot trefoil and clumps
of faded tiger lilies, her feet scaring up
toads the size of bees. Past the green
clothesline and around the garage.
At the edge of the drive rises a mound
of potted plants and smooth rocks,
a statue of Mary nestled among geraniums.
And before this, on the farm?
She wouldn't have had the luxury
of prayer for prayer's sake.
I imagine her folding prayers
into the clean laundry, tossing
prayer with hay into the summer
air with a pitchfork where it scatters
with chaff in the wind. Tugging
prayer from the black soil
where it clings to potatoes, forms
stubborn arcs under each fingernail.
She steers prayer across the field
in the tractor, shifts and brakes
and rock picks prayer till her back
is weary. Then she washes up
and fries prayer into the chicken,
chops it into the salad, whips it
into creamy mashed potatoes.
Bless us O Lord with these thy gifts
which we are about to receive.
Then out to the barn for the evening
milking, cats creeping close
as prayer froths and steams,
abundant, tired, overflowing.*

V.

A vase on the table holds water and fake flowers.
Grandma is in her new recliner,
its remote control as complicated
as the television's. "Those flowers
are from Rose," she says. "Rose left
on vacation and I said to myself, doggonit,
here she leaves me for a week and
doesn't tell me how I'm supposed to water
these flowers." I give my mom a look.
Grandma goes on about how hard it was
to fill the glass, carry it in the basket
of her walker, reach to the middle of the table
and pour. Then back to the kitchen
for more water. I imagine a small
Leinenkugel glass sloshing in her walker,
trembling in her hand as she reaches,
the water's trickle. I glance again at my mom.
Do we tell her the flowers aren't real?
Then Grandma grins—she's pulling our leg.
She'd wanted us to believe, as she had,
that the flowers were real, making light
of the anxiety that pushed her along all week
in her effort to keep them alive.
She settles back with a plucky laugh.
Less than an hour later, she tells me
the story again, not a joke this time.

e)

*For Grandma's ninetieth, we set up a tent
on the driveway to shelter the long table
where she sits with her sisters. Almost
all nine are still living, and their one
brother, too. A dozen years ago they traveled
to Poland, they found their father's
village and the house where he was born.
Sophie, the oldest, leads them in song
after song in Polish. They create a little
house out of music, its wood and stone
from words both strange and familiar,
its roof the top of the little tent, breathed
in and out by the breeze. We continue
our party around them, our cake and jokes,
our hula hoops and stories and too-much-food
accentuated by their laughter between songs.
A chorus of joyous old-woman cackles
flows into laughter from the rest of us,
ripples into new giggles when we hear
how similar my mom and her sisters sound.
Then an eruption of panicked, Oh-God-we're-next
laughter by me and the female cousins.
In the last bed-ridden weeks of Grandma's life,
Sophie will visit her, one hundred three years old,
still getting around with just a walker.
She'll sit on the edge of the bed and sing
the old songs, holding Grandma's hand
and stroking her head, her cheek.
She'll sooth her with her Polish name,
saying Róża, Róża. I'm here. I'm here.*

VI.

My mom and sister and I pull on long
socks and old shoes to go walking
on Grandma's land. Bloodroot
and trout lily. Peepers. Wild geranium.
Birches, and the staccato thump of a
courting grouse, more sensation
than sound. The pond is too low,
jagged with stumps and lumpy with
stretches of critter-tracked sand.
What will happen with this land?
Soon, we're crawling with ticks.
We pick them off socks, inseams, and
shoe tongues. Back at the house, we
strip down to our underwear
on the driveway, shake out shirts and pants.
Inside, Grandma wakes up in her chair.
"Someone stole our clothes!" I yell.
How good it feels, all of us laughing.
Some of the hard stuff that's collected
over the years floats down to the floor and,
like the ticks that keep crawling
from our clothes, gets flushed away.

f)

*Deer along the driveway
eating Grandma's apples,
those damn deer again
getting yelled at through
the screen. Deer in the yard,
deer in the garden, deer
in the corn, deer in the dark
with their eyes like moons.
Fawns with their kicks and
their spots and their nimble-
clumsy ways, bucks with their
points and does with cow-like
eyes. Cows with their lowing,
with their udders, with their teats,
cows with their eye rolls, with
their cud, with their fear, the cows
that escaped from the field
by the house, their hooves
traipsing past the basement
window when we woke.
Cows with their shit, with their
spots, with their wet velvet noses,
calves with their knees, with their
warm rough tongues. Call them
dumb, call them gentle, call them
poor beasts of burden. Call them
Bessie, call them home, see them
born in the mud. Cows
with their people, people with their
cows. Cows with their ear tags
and their flies, with their twitching
tails, twitching eyes. Cows
lying down in the field before rain.*

VII.

The three of us make dinner for the four of us.
Avocado appliances, dark wood,
clock with a dozen birds calling the hour.
We clear the oven of Grandma's thirteen
pieces of hardened toast spread with a thin
scrim of peanut butter, slide in fresh bread
wrapped in foil. And yet, *relish* is a word
to use between *my grandma* and
good food. The days of perfectly round
buttermilk pancakes, applesauce, and
raspberry preserves—all from scratch—
are a thing of the past. The breakfast
of back when. Now, we eat in the sun-
room, too light to close the blinds,
dusk deep enough for our reflections
to emerge in the glass. We dip bread
in garlic and olive oil, give Grandma
the choicest bits. It's nothing fancy:
pasta, broccoli, red wine poured by the
thimbleful in her glass. Her cheeks
are pink, her blunt fingers unsurprisingly
free of the slightest slick of olive oil.
She doesn't hear or understand
much of our conversation. Our images
saturate against the black-green
of the front yard and we repeat
ourselves, louder and slower, laugh
again in all the right places.
Later, Grandma will sing for us,
Froggy Went a Courtin', her chin
dipping and rising with each *mhmm*.
For now, she eats and eats.

g)

Each time I see you: new
age spots, darker, spreading
against your skin against
your will. I am ashamed
when I feel repulsed by a pale
flaky patch on your cheek.
You cannot help
the slow winding down
of the physical self. It houses
you still, each day another
light shone on the body's
slow demise. You are your body
and yet you are not.
You are, and you are not.
And when you are gone:
the next, and the next.
O Grandma, with your
strong soft hands
and your amber ring,
O humming, O humming,
O tidy, anxious ways.
How far we've come
without going anywhere.

VIII.

I don't fall asleep for fear of ticks
in the guise of moles on my back, ticks
buried in my crotch. The thermostat
is set to seventy-six. I've closed my door
and opened the window. In the night,
the slow creak of my grandma's walker
nudged down the hall, the scuff from carpet
to linoleum, the journey so slow
that I fall asleep and wake up repeatedly
before she makes it there and back again.
And again. And again. The night breeze
tugs the door open, lingers, bumps it shut.
I wake and wake to its endless percussion,
my mind stirred as if by something
I've forgotten and almost remembered.

h)

*I'm small enough to fit on the couch
beside the dining room table,
belly down, shins resting over
Grandma's thighs. It's the coveted
post-pajama-ing, pre-bed spot.
The lights are low, the fans are low,
the kitchen is clean.
The fine-ribbed corduroy
of the couch cushion, a slightly
pinkish brown-gray, is soft
and firm against my cheek.
Conversation washes over me—
my mom and her sisters with
subdued bursts of identical laughter,
an uncle or two dozing,
a few cousins, my brothers
and sister. Grandma smooths
her hands over my calves, slow
and repetitive. My brothers reenact
a scene from the day in their
dinosaur pajamas. We make
loose plans for tomorrow.
When the dishwasher stops,
I hear my grandma's skin
whispering over my own.
Back and forth, slow, back and forth.
Cricket song drifts through
the open sunroom doors.
Moths congregate on the screens.
In the dark, deer step unseen
through the wet grass, the yard
a different place entirely from where
I turned cartwheels under the sun.
My legs, strong and tan, are the most
real thing when I close my eyes,
my legs and my grandma's hands
folded into the voices weaving
and reaching through the air around us.*

IX.

The sunroom's morning light.
Every time I slide into downward dog,
Grandma calls some question
from the living room, only a few
high-pitched words audible—
shades up? Mom up? I give up
and start water for oatmeal.
A man from the church arrives,
white and round as the wafer
he's come to deliver.
They chat about the weather
and the news from town and the
weather as I scoop out coffee grounds.
It's hard to brew anything she likes now,
always *beastly hot* and *too damn strong*.
I'm poised to pour when the man's
voice slides into church service. I freeze.
To pour, or not to pour? My mom peeks
from the half bath where only I can see her,
wash cloth in hand, still wearing pajamas.
Bunny-like, she squinches up her nose.
We shake with silent laughter.
All those years in the country church,
on repeat in the kitchen: legs stuck
with sweat to the pew, windows tilted,
revealing in the beige wall a strip of green
and headstones, my family's dead,
the neighbors'. Up ahead, Mary demure
and close-lipped as ever, her glowing
heart and downcast eyes. Fans whir.
The priest's voice catches on the psalm
and someone—a sister, a cousin, an aunt—
presses fingers to lips, forearms to belly,
anything to keep the giggles in. Now,
with the smallest *clink*, I set the pot

on the counter and tip-toe-dart
to the half bath. It's tiny. Our faces
are red and contorted in the mirror.
Laughing, yes, but resembling
so many other strong emotions.
From the next room, the familiar litany
of the Our Father enters our held breath.
Then, the brief silence of Communion.

i)

A college friend says,
"Your grandma seems so sweet."
"She is," I say. "She even
teaches me Polish."
I recall her having me recite
a phrase to perfection
before telling me what it means.
"Okay, I've got it," I say,
repeating it one more time.
"Now what am I saying?"
Grandma throws back
her head and laughs.
"Go to hell," she says.
Grandma wears turtlenecks
and says you can start drinking
at eleven in the morning.
I'm told she used to kiss
my grandpa behind the ears—
or did he kiss her?
She was a couple inches
taller than him. One summer,
I take a photograph I find
face down in a dresser drawer.
Grandma and Grandpa
at somebody's house,
drinking beer across the counter.
A stainless steel sink
in the foreground, then
the two of them, relaxed,
smiling not at the camera
but in the glow of their own
thoughts. As if everyone
has just been laughing,

and now their private memories
of similar stories or shared
moments have risen from the depths
to meet them, comfortably, in this place.

X.

Later, I ask Grandma to tell me again
how all the Polish mamas would clutch
the coat sleeves of my not-yet grandpa
and say, "I have daughter for you!"
But he chose her. How, when they played
Roll out the Barrel, he went behind the bar,
and did. She remembers how he came in one day
after fifty-three years of marriage.
He stood at the edge of the counter holding
the mail where the linoleum meets the carpet,
behind him the chair from the old farmhouse
with hardened green leather cushions, a tall
metal frame, a footstool that clunks down to the floor.
During hunting season he'd come in after dark,
sit there in his bright orange. "Help Grandpa,"
my mom said once when I was five, showed me
how to tug down the coveralls. Grandma points.
"He was standing *right there*." He wore a cap,
his usual grin. He set the mail on the counter
and fell down with a heart attack and died.
"It was like life ended for me," she says.

j)

After Grandpa dies and Dad leaves,
Grandma comes to stay with us for the winter.
She trims loose threads when folding laundry
and joins our first Valentines picnic
on the family room floor. In third grade,
I'm downstairs alone in that room,
reading a book that slowly fills me with terror.
One light hovers above my left shoulder.
The rest of the house, from here, is dark.
I read and read because stopping is worse
than continuing on. Mom is upstairs
giving the baby a bath, my brother
and sister and grandma are up there, too.
I'm feeling lightheaded with fear when suddenly
a heavy globe light above the kitchen island
falls and shatters across the stove.
Of course, I don't identify the sound at the time.
A new sound enters my ears from far away, high-
pitched and elsewhere and endless. My throat hurts.
It is me, screaming. I know now
that I am screaming, but I am observing
this like a startled rabbit, not in control.
Somehow I arrive upstairs. All I know
is that my mom couldn't come to me,
but Grandma is there. I crawl under the covers
in the middle of Mom's big bed,
lie flat on my back with just my chin
poking out. Even in the dark, even in the numb
aftermath of my fear, I notice the way Grandma
lies down beside me, on top of the bedspread,
disturbing nothing, staying close.
An arm of light reaches from the closet across
her serene face, her clothes falling neat
and smooth, her hands folded quietly across her belly.

XI.

I pull my secret accordion
from the case I've smuggled
all the way from Michigan.
"Is that one hundred twenty keys?"
Grandma asks, and I tell her yes.
"That's just like mine was," she says.
She'd taken lessons briefly, then sold
the instrument—she didn't have time to play.
We're in the sunroom, my aunt and uncle
are here. I want to play my grandma a polka,
but I've hardly practiced, I'll trip on the chords.
My fingers tremble in the peachy light. I want
to take her back to a Saturday night,
the week's work finished, the moon
luxurious over the fields of sweet cut hay.
I want to take her back to the dance floor
jumping with the feet of a hundred polkas.
The sheer bliss of clasping hands
instead of cow teats, the thrill of twirling
in the arms of the man she loved, had made
a life with. Gravity loosened its grasp
on that little bar. Sometimes all you needed
to hold you up was another tune
with its counter melody of laughter,
scent of beer and sweat and the good
earth outside, the soil breathing in the dark.
G7, C Major. I play the polka, though not
very well—she doesn't recognize it.
The accordion grows heavy in my lap.
"It was a hard life, but a good life," she says.
And I feel our caught breath, our love,
reach out and hold her up. I squeeze
the last bit of air from the bellows.

k)

In the Blue Hills beyond
the old farm falls
the Felsenmeer,
sea of rock, V of
rocks forever sliding
since the last glacier
heaved itself through.
In the heat of July,
the entrance to the great
rock mouth of crumbling
teeth exudes cool,
damp air. The refrigeration
of centuries seeping
up and up from endless
rock below. We pause
a moment in the earth's
cold breath. Then we pick
our way through the center,
rock to rock, lichen
and angles and slide and
shift. Each time, it feels
as if no time has passed.
The same old rocks
and the familiar crossing.
One year, in the
leaf heavy woods
early in our quest,
we're frozen by the liquid
trill of a bird
we've never heard before.
O beauty and color somewhere
above, mysterious bird
we never see. That one call,
and we never hear it again.

XII.

Someone remembers the pack of photographs.
They're from Grandpa's half-brother
to my grandma, years ago. "My new condo,"
his note reads. "Sit back and enjoy."
He'd chronicled his kitchen cabinets,
the living room fan, the dining room fan,
the bathroom fan, the music station with
minuscule stereo and 3D jesters jouncing
on the wall. We're crying, we're laughing
so hard. The pictures contain everything
and capture nothing. A sink. A pantry.
My new place: a blank brick wall.
My mom steps closer to her mom,
who leans too far in her chair.
We keep flipping through pictures,
wiping away tears. One photo features
a cement slab and chain link, a statue
of Mary chipping blue. "Fence, patio,
Blessed Virgin," the caption reads.
As if arranging the perfect scene
could keep her there always.

In loving memory of Rose Angeline Czyscon Antczak
July 14, 1918 – August 18, 2016

Kristin Brace writes poetry, fiction, and children's literature. She also serves as executive director of the Grand Rapids Creative Youth Center, where kids become published authors. Brace earned an MFA in Writing from Spalding University and her work has appeared in journals such as *Fiction Southeast, The Louisville Review, Water~Stone, The Chariton Review,* and *The Other Journal.* Brace plays the accordion, studies Italian, and loves Lake Michigan in every season. She makes her home in West Michigan with her husband, the entrepreneur and inventor Neal Brace. Though she knew she wanted to be a writer at age five, *Fence, Patio, Blessed Virgin* is her first book.

www.ingramcontent.com/pod-product-compliance
Lightning Source LLC
LaVergne TN
LVHW041519070426
835507LV00012B/1678